Vintage In
Birmingham /

CW00802819

by
Andrew Maxam

No. 3 in a series featuring photographs and postcards from the twentieth century

1. Old Crown, 188 & 189 High Street, Deritend / Heath Mill Lane, c1955. Not, as legend has it, a pub from dating from 1368, but originally built in the late 15th century, c1480, as the Guildhall and School of the Guild of St. John the Baptist of Deritend. The decorative tie-beams are comparable to an example at the Saracen's Head at King's Norton, datable to 1492. The earliest authenticated deed relating The Crown to an (un-named) inn is dated 1589 and two hundred years later is the first reference to it being called the Old Crown. Bought by Holts Brewery at auction in 1925, it later became an Ansells tied house. Extensive renovations had been carried out, first in 1862, when the ground floor was rebuilt in brick. After closure for five years, other alterations were carried out in 1998 when the north extension was converted to bedrooms and a rear entrance was added. This is the only complete surviving mediaeval building in Birmingham, excluding villages now incorporated into the city, and is Grade II* listed.

Ansells Brewery – A Brief History

In 1857, Joseph Ansell commenced production as a maltster at the junction of Lichfield Road and Park Road, Aston Cross, Birmingham. This was the site of seven artesian wells. In 1864, he was joined by his son William and in 1876 another son Edward joined the growing partnership which became Joseph Ansell & Sons. Records show that in those early days, they erected new malt houses, acquired a new site at Moseley Road and included hop merchants as part of their activities. In 1881, they turned their attention to brewing. Joseph died in 1885 and, under the guidance of his sons and head brewer, the firm was converted into a limited company, Ansell & Sons Ltd. From 1889 to 1901, the brewery was enlarged several times and the number of public houses grew from 96 in 1889 to 388 in 1901. A bottling plant was also installed. Once again, the company needed refinancing and a new company, Ansells Brewery Ltd was formed in 1901. William died in 1904 and was succeeded by Edward as Chairman. During World War 1, the company struggled, as many did, due to supply shortages and restrictions, higher costs, diminished output and high taxes. In 1919, Edward resigned the Chairmanship in favour of his son Harry Ansell, only to resume office again in 1920 after his son's untimely death.

In 1889, Ansells had taken over Edward Cartwright's Brewery based at Birchfield; then in 1911 they took over King & Barton; in 1923 the local Rushton's Brewery (which added more than 300 public houses). Lucas of Leamington Spa also succumbed in 1928. When Edward died in 1929, the last link with the Ansell family ended. The Holt Brewery, based at Holt Street, Gosta Green was taken over in 1934 and added another 250 licensed houses, making Ansells one of the largest brewery pub estates in the country. Holts' squirrel motif was incorporated into the Ansells logo. Holts continued production as Ansells No. 2 brewery until the early 1970s. The faint Holt Brewery lettering can still be seen on the Gosta Green pub. In 1939, the rebuilding of the main Brewery commenced, a task not completed until the 1950s, well after the war ended.

In 1961, Ansells merged with Tetley Walker and Ind Coope to form Allied Breweries (later Allied Domecq then Punch Retail Ltd). By the late 1960s, Ansells controlled over 2,500 public houses. A series of notorious strikes in the 1970s and early 1980s meant that Allied closed Aston Brewery in 1981 and moved production to the Ind Coope site at Burton-upon-Trent. Ansells Bitter and Mild were never quite the same again. Currently, these beers are brewed by J W Lees at Manchester. Four ex Ansells employees formed the Aston Manor Brewery at Thimble Mill Lane, Aston in 1983. They now concentrate on cider production.

Two of the most notable pubs Ansells owned over the years were the Old Crown at Deritend (believed to be an inn since 1589 and the Green Man or (Old) Lad in the Lane, Bromford Lane, Erdington, which has been proved to date from 1400.

Foreword by Professor Carl Chinn MBE

Andrew Maxam is one of a small group of people who not only are passionate about Birmingham's history but also are passionate about bringing that past to a wider audience. That deeply-held belief in sharing knowledge, photographs, postcards, memorabilia and whatever else is a vital one. Often we read of priceless works of art disappearing into the vaults of wealthy collectors who want only that they themselves can gaze at the beauty of what they have bought. In effect such a selfish action imprisons that artistic achievement, stifles it, and denies it the opportunity to reach out to peoples of different backgrounds and bring them together. Andrew is not such a person. For many years he has collected images of old Birmingham and for as long he has generously shared them with other researchers. Those images of Ansells pubs can now be shared with an even wider audience. I congratulate Andrew on his achievement.

Contents

2. Pot of Beer, Holt Street / Lister Street, Gosta Green, 8.1.1989. Built within the old Holts Brewery offices, with the former brewery being known as Ansells No. 2 Brewery. The Pot opened as Ansells tap house on 29.7.1969, receiving a licence from the Grand Turk, Hockley Hill which had closed in 1965. In the 1990s it was renamed Faculty & Firkin. It was later bought by Mitchells & Butlers as part of the Scream chain aimed at students and was renamed the Gosta Green. The Scream chain was sold to new pub company, Stonegate in 2010.

Chapter 1 City Centre

3. Golden Eagle, 106 Hill Street / Swallow Street, 1985, after closure. This distinctive polished black granite building replaced an earlier inn (since at least 1855) and was built for Holts by the architect Frank Osborne, a year after the Ansells take over in 1935. An engraved Golden Eagle used to preside over the front door and a circular staircase led to the Assembly Room. The interior bar front

and back featured light wooden panelling and zigzag patterns on the mirror-glass – very Art Deco. A former licensee told the author of the sadness everyone felt when it closed due to structural defects. It had a reputation for live music and was a bikers' pub. The site is now occupied by a car park but a little of the black granite finishing still survives as a memento on Hill Street. Henry's (later Victoria's, now Chameleon Bar) replaced it further up the hill.

4. Grapes Hotel, 78 Hill Street / Severn Street as featured on a postcard in 1908. Dating from 1840, it was acquired by Manchester Brewery Co in 1898 who were then taken over by Ansell's. A new house was built in 1938 by John P Osborne & Co, the same architects who were respon-

sible for the Golden Eagle, and there were similarities in its look. The Grapes closed in 1966 and was again rebuilt to a very plain design. It was renamed Metropolis then Hill Street Q's in the 1980s before closing in 2004 for conversion to a supermarket.

5. Bull's Head, 1 Price Street / 41&42 Loveday Street, c1936. Set in what was Birmingham's Gun Quarter, the first recorded licensee was Joseph Showell in 1812 though there was thought to be a gun maker and beer retailer here as early as 1729. Now known as the Bull, it has been a regular entry in the CAMRA Good Beer Guide for many years.

6. Longboat, Cambrian Wharf, Kingston Row, c1979. It opened 3.2.1970 overlooking the then run-down Cambrian Wharf. The pub took its licence from the former Cambridge Inn in nearby Cambridge Street which had closed 21.1.1968. It was taken over by the Firkin chain in the 1990s when its name changed to the Flapper and Firkin; since abbreviated to the Flapper.

7. Eagle & Tun, 46 New Canal Street / Banbury Street, 1985. Purchased by Ansells for £1,500 in 1897, this James & Lister Lea-designed terracotta pub was rebuilt in 1900, replacing an inn that had been on the site since at least 1845. It was renamed the Cauliflower Ear in the late 1980s before sensibly reverting back to its original name. It featured in the Birmingham reggae band UB40's Red Red Wine video in 1990 and on album cover, Best of UB40, Volume 2 in 1995. Although the pub closed in 2008, it is hoped that this pub will reopen.

8. Salutation Inn, 86 Snow Hill / Summer Lane, 1961. There was a pub on this site from at least 1750 when the ancient sport of bull-baiting used to take place in this area. In the early 19th century, the Salutation was said to present a "countrified" appearance, with a quaint porch and outside benches. Rebuilt c1887 by architect William Jenkins, Holts bought it in 1904. By the 1960s it had a reputation for live jazz as well as boxing. It closed for demolition in 1968 and the site remained vacant for many years. The last licensee was the father of the current lanlord at the Anchor on Bradford Street. The site of the Salutation was only developed in recent years and is now occupied by housing.

9. Red Lion Waverley Hotel, 10 & 11 New Meeting Street and 58 High Street, 22.10.1968. Existing on this site since 1780, its frontage was originally where "Stylo" shoe shop is in High Street, but by the time of this picture its entrance was confined to New Meeting Street. This was a popular bar and smoke room, also known as the Vaults. By 1976 it was described in a pub guide as "easily the tattiest bar in the city centre but with a certain down-trodden maudlin charm." In 1977, plans were afoot to redevelop it and despite much opposition, in 1980 it was replaced by a two storey shopping block which currently includes a McDonald's restaurant.

6

10. Prince of Wales, 84 Cambridge Street, 1967. This Victorian beerhouse dates from 1852 and the site once formed part of the grounds of Bingley House, the home of the Lloyds banking family. Bought by Holts in 1887. After extensive renovation, it re-opened as the Prince of Wales public house, In 1934, the Prince became an Ansells tied house. Under threat of demolition in the mid 1980s, it was saved and incorporated into the International Convention Centre complex after a high profile campaign. Many people remember the rare Holts squirrel trademark etched glass in the snug, removed in the 1998 Festival Alehouse harsh refurbishment which knocked all the rooms into one and repositioned the bar. It has been a regular entry in the Birmingham CAMRA Good Beer Guide since 1975.

11. Oddfellows Arms, 135 Sherlock Street, 1936. This early Victorian beerhouse was purchased by Ansells by public auction in 1899. It became a fully licensed house, i.e able to sell wines and spirits, in 1937. It traded under a variety of names in the 1990s and 2000s including Den, Gorgeous and Rebellion. The 3 storey building is still standing today.

12. Fox, 54 & 56 Hurst Street / Inge Street, opposite the Hippodrome Theatre, c 1935; now known as the Old Fox. A pub has been established here since at least 1813. In the 1860s, it was known as the Fox and Freemasons' Tavern. Holts Brewery commissioned the architects James & Lister Lea to rebuild the pub in 1892. It is alleged that Charlie Chaplin drank here and various theatrical items adorn the walls. It is a regular entry in the CAMRA Good Beer Guide.

13. Bingley Hall Hotel, 16 King Alfred's Place, c1959. This former Showells Brewery / Ind Coope pub dates from at least 1851 and stood opposite Bingley Hall. It closed for trading 20.1.1965 and its licence was removed to the Albatross in Castle Bromwich which opened in 1968. Following redevelopment, this site is now occupied by the International Convention Centre and King Alfred's Place no longer exists.

14. Coach and Horses, 30 Snow Hill, 1959. This narrow-fronted four storey Georgian building dated from c1800 when it was first known as the Lord Wellington. It was taken over by Ansells in the 1890s. By the 1950s, this was a rundown area and in 1961 the pub, along with other buildings on the east side of Snow Hill facing the railway station, was demolished for construction of the Inner Ring Road.

Chapter 2 Digbeth and Deritend

15. Dog Inn, 154 Alcester Street, situated between Moseley Street & Cheapside, 1967. Dating from before the 1860s, it was acquired by Ansells in 1924. The cellar was accessed through the trap door in front of the counter of the small single bar, resulting in chaos when beer was delivered. It closed in 1983 and for many years was used by the Light House Rescue Mission. Currently the building is in use as a fish and chip shop and there is still evidence of the now painted-out Ansell's sign, far left.

16. Spotted Dog, 104 Warwick Street / Alcester Street, 1986, A pub has been on this site since 1865. Ansells bought it and subsequently rebuilt it. One of two Spotted Dog pubs in the vicinity, it is now a traditional Irish freehouse. It has been an occasional entry in the CAMRA Good Beer Guide.

17. Smithfield Arms, 47 Jamaica Row, right, in the heart of the old Bull Ring Markets area. Dating from 1885, the architects were James & Lister Lea who designed it In Queen Anne style. It closed in 1970 for development of the Wholesale Markets which resulted in the loss of dozens of pubs in the area.

18. Anchor, 308 Bradford Street / Rea Street, c1936. Ansells bought the Anchor in 1889 and this red brick and terracotta James & Lister Lea two storey building was built in 1902, replacing an inn that had been in existence since at least 1829. It is Grade II listed and on the CAMRA National Inventory of Historic Pub Interiors. Renowned for its remarkably intact interior including a rare surviving timber and glass screen dividing the main public bar into two, as well as original bar back and cut-glass mirrors and Art Nouveau style stained glass. It has been run by the Keane family since 1973 and upon surrender of the lease by Ansells in 1994, it became a freehouse. Regular winner of Birmingham CAMRA awards, including Pub of the Year.

19. Dog & Partridge, 210/2 Moseley Street / 51 Birchall Street, c1970. The bar at this impressive James & Lister Lea tile and terracotta, Grade II listed pub from 1899-1900, (replacing an earlier inn). It is listed in the CAMRA National Inventory of Historic Pub Interiors and has a superb tiled stairway hall. A fire in 1984 gutted the upper two storeys and in 1986 it was reopened after repairs and restoration, renamed The Market Tavern. It became a popular live music venue. Sadly closed since 2008, it is hoped it will eventually reopen.

Chapter 3 Acocks Green and Hall Green

20. New Inn, Westley Road Shirley Road / Acocks Green, 1932, shortly after the pub was rebuilt to serve this rapidly-expanding area. It replaced an inn which had been situated at 1099 Warwick Road since mid Victorian times. In recent years, it has traded under various names such as Beagles Flies Again, Lloyds on the Green, Lafferty's and, since 2003, Inn on the Green.

21. Dog & Partridge, 146 Priory Road, c1995. Another large inter-war pub rebuilt to serve the rapidly expanding residential areas of Hall Green and Yardley Wood. A pub has been situated on this site since before the 1860s. It closed as a pub in 1997 and is now in use as a Haven Church, a trend that is increasingly common as a further use for redundant Birmingham pubs.

22. Horseshoe Inn, 1214 Stratford Road, between School Road and Staplehurst Road, Hall Green, as depicted on a postcard posted in 1910. A former beerhouse dating from at least 1869, it was added to the Ansells estate in 1926. Note the then rural aspect of the surroundings. At one stage it was renamed Toad Hall, before reverting to the Horseshoe. In 2008, it was extensively modernised internally

Chapter 4 Ashted, Bloomsbury, Duddeston, Nechells & Vauxhall

23. Beehive, 342 Bloomsbury Street / Nechells Place. High Park Corner, 1965, with Saltley Gasworks in the background. This fully licensed house was purchased by Ansells in 1900 for £4,500 though it had been trading for many years before. The pub closed 30.11.1966 and the area was totally redeveloped.

24. Turk's Head, 150 Bloomsbury Street / Saltley Road, Hyde Park Corner, 1960. This mid nineteenth century pub was purchased by Ansells for £2,750 in 1900. Note the splendid clock tower of the surviving Bloomsbury Library, far right. The M & B pub just visible above the bus, far left distance, was the Brewery Tavern on the corner of Cranbury Street. The Turk's Head closed 25.2.1961 and its licence went into suspense until removed to the Pelican at Hockley which opened in 1965. All this area has been redeveloped.

25. Red Lion, 272 Thimble Mill Lane / High Park Street, 1966. Dated from around 1855, when William Ford was recorded as a retail brewer. This former Holts pub closed in 1967 and its licence was transferred to a new pub, the Dukes, in the basement of the Grosvenor Shopping Centre at Northfield. All this area was cleared and the lane was upgraded to a busy dual carriageway. Nowadays this area is dominated by a large Chinese supermarket.

26. Adelaide Arms, 159 Vauxhall Road / Erskine Street, photographed in 1968 shortly before closure and demolition. This pub dated from pre-1855. Ansells surrendered the licence in 1969. The site now forms part of an extension of St. Vincent's Catholic Primary School.

Chapter 5 Aston

27. Vine, 157 Lichfield Road / Sandy Lane & Park Street, c1930. Dating from the 1840s and said to be the only pub in Birmingham built on "a road, a lane and a street." Apart from rendering over the brickwork, it has altered little externally, with even the Lichfield Road sign remaining to this day though the surrounding terraced housing and old cast iron urinals, once a common sight, have long since gone.

28. Swan Pool Tavern, 305 Lichfield Road / Holborn Hill, as pictured on a postcard sent in 1908, when still a Holts pub. Rebuilt in 1898 by architects James and Lister Lea; in the 1870s it was called The Station Inn. Under threat of road widening in the 1970s, it became run down and in 1984, it was vandalised by football fans. In 1985 it was extensively refurbished and renamed the Swan & Mitre.

29. Bricklayers Arms, 233 Clifton Road / Potter's Hill, shown in the late 1960s when a delivery of large wooden beer barrels was taking place. This fully licensed pub was in existence by 1869, and closed at the end of 1971. Both sections of these streets have now disappeared and new housing now occupies this site.

30. Aston Tavern, 10 Aston Hall Road, 7.9.1960. Purchased by Ansells in 1898 for £2,500, the pub was rebuilt in 1904 (replacing an inn dating from at least 1845. It is typical of others in the area with colourful tiling and etched windows. This area is now dominated by the roar of the Aston Expressway which passes nearby. The pub closed in 1996 and the building still stands, now sadly in a derelict state, its future uncertain.

31. General Wolfe, 23 Aston Road / Love Lane, 1967. A pub had been on this site since before 1820 and was named after General James Wolfe, commander of the British Forces that defeated the French at Quebec in 1759. The pub closed for demolition 14.1.1986. Aston University campus has encroached into this area, This part of Aston Road has been renamed Holt Street.

Chapter 6 Balsall Heath, Highgate, King's Heath, Moseley & Yardley Wood

32. Wellington, Mary Street / Balsall Heath Road, 1967. This pub was trading since the early 1800s and was one of 10 pubs or beerhouses on Mary Street. In the 1910s, it was named the Criterion, an early example of a chain pub group as were several other pubs. such as the Sir Charles Napier on Gooch Street and Duke of York, Harborne. The Wellington closed on 16.1.1975 and has now been demolished and the site grassed over.

33. Woodman, Edward Road / Lincoln Street, Balsall Heath, 1975. This mid nineteenth century former beerhouse closed on 25.7.1977 due to a compulsory purchase order by the Council. Every trace of this scene has now gone, replaced by housing, set further back from the road. The Lincoln Street road sign that used to be attached to the pub did survive though, having been attached to a nearby fence!

34. Prince of Wales, 91 Angelina Street / Stanhope Street, Highgate, 20.11.1957. This beerhouse had been trading since the 1860s. The two steps on Angelina Street led to the door to the Bar on the right. Note the derelict state of some of the adjacent housing. The Prince closed for demolition in 1960 and its site is now occupied by a School Academy.

35. Plough & Harrow, 195 Moseley Road, adjacent to the Alhambra Cinema, Highgate, 1960. It dated back to the 1820s. This Georgian house received a late Victorian extension to the front. Entrance to the bar was on the left, while the outdoor was accessed via the middle door. It closed for trading 27.7.1969, with the cinema following in 1974 for demolition. This section of Moseley Road is now a dual carriageway.

36 & 37. Hare and Hounds, High Street / York Road, King's Heath, c1912 (exterior) & 1975 (interior). It was rebuilt in 1907 by then-owner Charles Collett which replaced an earlier, smaller inn from the 1820s. Collett sold it to Holts in 1910 and, despite many alterations and refurbishments over the years, it still retains a myriad of coloured Maw tiling. It is Grade II listed but not on CAMRA's National Inventory.

38. Station, 7 High Street, King's Heath, 1985. Dating from 1889, the first licensees were recorded as William and Elizabeth Frost. It faced what was Kings Heath railway station which was in existence from 1867 to 1941. The Station pub (also referred to as the Station Hotel) still trades today and attractive tiling adorns some internal passageways.

39. Prince of Wales, 118 Alcester Road, Moseley, 1985. This famous local has been at the heart of Moseley life since 1861 and is rumoured to have been used by local author J.R.R. Tolkien. Unlike many pubs, its suite of rooms have not been knocked into one over the years. The Prince now now boasts an impressive beer garden suitable for live music. Long-serving licensees Bill and Bridget Halloran ran the Prince from 1963-1995.

40. Warstock, 1142 Yardley Wood Road / Prince of Wales Lane. Ansells purchased the freehold of this huge site in 1926 for the considerable sum of £19,200. This 1930s postcard shows a recently built Warstock. It closed in 2000 and was demolished to make way for the Waterways Court apartments. Amazingly the pub sign stand has survived!

Chapter 7 Bordesley & Bordesley Green

41. Ship Hotel, Camp Hill / Sandy Lane c1930. This 1870s three-storey building replaced a much earlier inn, originally named the Anchor, which contained an oak beam dated 1560. Legend has it this was the headquarters of Prince Rupert, prior to his assault on Birmingham in 1643. Acquired by Ansells in 1897, it was to close 13.4.1971 for demolition due to road widening of this junction.

42. Barrel Inn, 185 Watery Lane / Kingston Road, c1936. At this time the pub, which dated from 1862, had custom-made engraved glass. By the 1950s, the Barrel had received a facelift and looked quite strikingly different with stone cladding and arched upper windows. Closed in 1981, the Barrel was later demolished as part of the Watery Lane Middleway road widening scheme and the site is now occupied by a car showroom.

43. Waggon & Horses, 29 Adderley Street, c1978. Dates from c1835. When Ansells merged with Ind Coope in 1961, it became an Ansell's pub. Sold by Ansell's in 1986, for a while it became a jazz club, renamed The Cannonball, named after the jazz musician Julian "Cannonball" Adderley, a member of the Miles Davis Quintet. Its name reverted back to the Waggon and still is open for trading today, relatively unaltered externally.

44. Acorn, 119 Garrison Lane / Barwell Road, c1978. The Acorn was a beerhouse that dated from the mid 1800s. In the background under the Ansells sign, the tower of the Sportsman can just be seen. The Acorn displays typical Ansells signage for this time. It closed on 22.5.1983 due to a compulsory purchase order by the Council. Housing now occupies this site as part of an urban renewal scheme for this area and Barwell Road has been truncated.

45. Marquis of Lorne, 133 Cattell Road / Arsenal Street, c1935. It was named after John Campbell, 9th Duke of Argyll and the 4th Governor of Canada, who married Queen Victoria's daughter, Louise. Ansells first took a lease out on this pub in 1896. In 2009 the pub was renamed "The Roost" and is still open for trading.

Chapter 8 Erdington, Perry Common & Kingstanding

46. Roe Buck Inn, 132 & 134 High Street, Erdington, c1925. This building, boasting three billiard tables and a bowling green at rear, replaced an earlier inn dating back to 1760 (originally named the Bull's Head). In turn, this building closed in 1965 and was replaced by a modern, plain building which opened in 1966 as part of the High Street improvement. It was later renamed Posers, Old Roebuck, before closure. It reopened in 2011 as part of the Hairy Lemon chain.

47. Ye Olde Green Man (now renamed by its earlier nickname, The Lad in the Lane), 22 Bromford Lane, c1936, after a substantial refurbishment. Due to tree-ring testing (dendrochronology), it has been proven to be Birmingham's oldest pub building, with some surviving timbers dating back to Spring 1400, beating the Old Crown by approximately 80 years. It has been a pub since c1780 and is a Grade II listed building.

48. Golden Cross, Short Heath Road / Turfpits Lane, c1928. Architecturally typical for its time when it was originally built for Holts in the 1920s. It was a popular live music venue in the 1960s. In the 1990s it became an Irish themed bar, renamed O'Shea's, before closing in the early 2000s. The building was demolished in 2005 and the site is now occupied by a large development of flats.

49. College Arms, College Road / Warren Farm Road, c1936. This dates from c1930 and is a typical example of a suburban roadhouse favoured by Ansells in this period. This area was built up in the late 1920s after the owner of the Perry Hall estate sold his land to Birmingham Corporation for housing, as part of the North Birmingham Town Planning Scheme. The architect was Holland W Hobbiss (see also page 35, Fox & Goose, Ward End). The College's licence was surrendered 9.3.1994 and it became a McDonald's restaurant, a fate that has befallen the former Broadway pub at Bordesley Green and the Cartland Arms at King's Norton (both formerly Mitchells & Butlers pubs).

Chapter 9 Handsworth, Lozells & Perry Barr

50. Villa Cross Hotel, 243 Lozells Road / Heathfield Road / Villa Road, c1924. There has been a public house at this site for at least 150 years. This former Holts pub was rebuilt in the late 1930s. Members of the Birchfield Harriers used to meet here. After its close association with the Handsworth Riots of 1985, it closed in 1986 and is now in use as an Employment Centre.

51. Farcroft Hotel, Rookery Road / Onibury Road & Albion Road, as depicted on a postcard from the 1920s. This massive public house was originally built by Holts Brewery in 1923 in what became known as "Brewers Tudor style". Renowned for its barbecues and as a wedding and banqueting venue, the Farcroft is still open today.

52. Village Maid, 10 Finch Road, 1985. This early Victorian beer-house's freehold was purchased by Ansells in 1921 from a Mrs Brookes for £4,000. A popular local, its licence was not renewed 2.2.2001 due to objections by West Midlands Police. Now demolished, the site is a car park of a National Health Service Care Centre.

53. Lozells Inn, 67/69 Lozells Road, c1936. An inn has existed on this site since the 1840s. Note the elaborate electric Lozells Inn pub sign, in addition to painted boards prevalent in those days. Its licence was not renewed 12.2.1998 and the building is now used as a shop, with a painted Ansell's sign still visible.

54. Boar's Head Inn, Aldridge Road, Perry Barr was originally built in 1758. This postcard shows a 19th century building which stood until 1937 when it was demolished and replaced by the present building which is now closed and boarded up. The inn's name comes from the heraldic crest of the Gough family of Perry Hall. This scene is more tranquil compared to the roar of the M6 motorway nearby!

Chapter 10 Harborne

55. Old House at Home, 193 Lordswood Road / Gillhurst Road, c1928. In 1913, this large roadhouse replaced the smaller, former Rushton's inn that stood further down Lordswood Road towards Bearwood. The replacement premises were built on the site of a former football ground and remains a popular food-orientated pub.

56. Golden Cross, 215 Metchley Lane / Harborne Park Road, c1936. A superb interior view of the then recently rebuilt Golden Cross. The licensees were Mr and Mrs Thomas F Hadley. Renamed The Lazy Fox in the 1980s, then the Florence & Firkin, thankfully it reverted to its original name after a concerted campaign by The Harborne Society. It became part of the Arena chain of pubs and closed in 2008 and was demolished in December 2010. It was replaced by doctors' and nurses' flats to serve the new Queen Elizabeth Hospital.

57. White Horse, 2 York Street, c 1968 when plans were afoot to replace the plain Ansell's logo pub sign with a pictorial sign. This former beerhouse dates from the 1860s. It is a highly popular side street pub near the High Street and has recently become a freehouse.

58 & 59. King's Head, Hagley Road / Lordswood Road on the border with Bearwood, c1958 and c1975. Built by Holts in 1905, replacing an earlier inn. A stained glass panel recorded that the pub was licensed in the reign of George III (1760-1820). The architects were Owen & Ward who were also responsible for the original Alexandra Theatre. A faint Holt's sign is still visible today on the roof, looking from the Lordswood Road side. The clock, far left, was removed in the late 1960s due to road widening and now stands at the junction of Union Street and High Street in Birmingham City Centre. Renamed Quantum in the 1990s. Following a period of closure in the 2000s when a road scheme threatened demolition, the King's Head reopened under its original name after a substantial refurbishment in 2007. The interior view from 1975 shows the smoke room, which featured tiled framed tile paintings depicting English castles. These were later replaced by mirrors. Some fine Maw coloured tiling still remains today in the staircase area.

Chapter 11 Hockley

60. Black Eagle, 16 Factory Road, Soho, c1935. This building dates from 1895, replacing a brewhouse first recorded in 1856 on premises built in the 1770s. Threatened with closure in 1988, it was rescued by former actor Tony Lewis in 1990 who has run the Black Eagle for over 20 years. This old-fashioned community local stands out as a gem in a grimly industrial area. Its traditional beer garden is outstanding. A regular entry in CAMRA's Good Beer Guide and multi-winner of the Pub of the Year category.

61. Church Inn, 22 Great Hampton Street / Harford Street, c1936. The Church is believed to have taken its name from the nearby St. George's Church, which was demolished due to dry rot in 1960. Established by 1845, the Church has served many businesses that had sprung up on the fringe of the Jewellery Quarter. Still open today.

62. Trees Inn, 9 Hockley Hill / York Terrace, 1934, in the days when billiards and pool were played upstairs. The Trees dates from the early nineteenth century. Ansells acquired this house plus the adjoining property in 1924 for £6,500. Note the mixture of painted and individual character Ansells signs. Later, a fake marble cladding was applied to the lower storey. The Trees closed in the mid 1980s and is now in use as a Car Audio shop.

63. St. George's Vaults, 157 Great Hampton Row / Unett Street, 1958. Dating from at least 1829 when it was known as St. George's Stores. Its nickname was the three XXX's though it took its name from the nearby St. George's Church, like the Church Inn (61). This small Regency-style beerhouse closed c1959 as this area was rebuilt in the early 1960s, with the Little Brown Jug pub (M&B) opening on the diagonally opposite corner in 1964. Note the painted Ansells signage.

Chapter 12 King's Norton, Selly Oak & Stirchley

64. Camp Inn, 1 Camp Lane / Station Road, King's Norton, c1950. In the early to mid 20th century it was known as the Railway or New Railway Inn. A former beerhouse at 10 Camp Lane had been in existence since at least 1869. Some 1920s wooden panelling inside still gives this pub a traditional feel.

65. Plough & Harrow, 759 Bristol Road / Chapel Lane, c1905. Dating from 1900, this Holts (later Ansells) hostelry was known as the New Inn until 1904. It closed 4.3.1983, subject of a compulsory purchase order by the Council for the Bristol Road widening scheme. Note the Dog & Partridge, selling Butlers ales, opposite, also now demolished.

66. Breedon Cross Hotel, 1652 Pershore Road / Lifford Lane, 1996, a year after it had its licence revoked. A pub had been on this site from at least the 1860s. In later years it was often referred to as the Breedon Bar and was renowned as a live music venue. As can be seen, it suffered fire damage and was eventually demolished in 2003; the site is now occupied by housing.

Chapter 13 Ladywood & Lee Bank

67. Cross Keys, 81 Steward Street, 1954. Licensee Samuel Brindley was recorded as a retail brewer here in 1855. In 1901 Ansells paid £825 for this small beerhouse that has still managed to keep going over the years. It is now much modernised internally.

68. Steam Clock, 23 Morville Street / Sherborne Street, c1954. This distinctive building is dated 1893 in the terracotta in the gable and it was also a music hall. It closed for demolition 17.10.1954, an early victim of the many beerhouses and pubs that were lost as this area was completely rebuilt. Its licence went into suspense until its removal to the Ashmeadow at King's Heath, which opened in 1959.

69. Vine, 1 Rawlins Street / Ruston Street. Trading as a beerhouse by 1850 but in 1855 the premises were named the Vine Inn when this area of Birmingham was known as Islington (hence Islington Row nearby). One the oldest buildings still standing in this area that was rebuilt in the 1960s when all the old back to back houses were demolished.

70. Belle Vue Inn or Hotel, 289 Icknield Port Road / Wiggin Street, 22.2.1967, with Henry Wiggin's metal factory next door. A pub has been on this site since the mid nineteenth century. This building was an inter-war rebuild. The entrance to the Smoke Room was through the door on the left, with the centre door being for off sales. Its licence was revoked 6.2.1997. The building still stands and bears the name of the pub despite being converted to housing.

71. Stour Valley Inn, 116 Monument Road / Gt. Tindal Street, 4.3.1961. This fully-licensed house has existed from the 1830s when this section of Monument Road was known as Icknield Street West. Closed 26.9.1962 as this whole area was cleared for redevelopment.

72. Ingleby Arms, 24 Ingleby Street, 1962. This fully licensed house dated from the early Victorian era. This view features it with a 1930s-style frontage. It closed 2.1.1966 for redevelopment. Ingleby Street was one of many Ladywood streets that were lost forever during the 1960s redevelopment.

73. Bull's Head, 38 Bishopsgate Street / Tennant Street, c1936. A typical James & Lister Lea tile and terracotta pub from 1901, replacing an older inn that dated from c1788. It later passed to Highgate Brewery of Walsall and when closed for refurbishment, the original bar back and snob screens were stolen. Now renamed the City Tavern and has Grade II listed status. It was rebranded under the former brewery, Davenports brand in 2009. The original Davenports brewery stood nearby at Bath Row.

74. White Swan, 57 Grosvenor Street West, 1985. This former beerhouse dated from at least 1869 and was rebuilt in the 1920s. The long front bar and bar back are still intact. In the early 2000s, it was renamed Darwin's though subsequently it has reverted to its original name and survives to this day.

75. Colmore Arms, 85 Latimer Street. This fully licensed house dated from at least 1855. Closed 2.12.1963 and even the street has disappeared as part of the 1960s Lee Bank redevelopment. Demolition appears underway in this c1959 view.

Chapter 14 Newtown

76. Fountain Inn, 327 Farm Street, 1961. Dating from at least 1855 when John Wiseman is recorded as a retail brewer. The pub closed 1.2.1966 as the old housing was cleared and replacement housing now occupies this site.

77. Crown Inn, 95 Villa Street / Nursery Road, January 1968. The building dates from the mid nineteenth century and is in Ansells livery more akin from a much earlier era. Note the extended frontage, from the late Victorian era. The pub closed at the end of 1968 for demolition. Housing now occupies this site.

78. Marquis of Lorne, Cecil Street / 40&42&44 New Town Row. This imposing former Holts pub was rebuilt on the site of an earlier inn c1903 to the designs of architect C H Collett who was also responsible for the Church Tavern on Lichfield Road, Aston. Boxing matches used to take place here. It closed in 1963 and was demolished due to subsequent road widening of New Town Row. Its licence was removed to the Harriers, Broadway, Perry Barr which opened in 1968.

79. Porchester Arms, 96 Porchester Street / Clifford Street, c1960. Looking rather run down, this back street boozer had such a small smoke room that it was a full house if a dozen punters came in. It closed in 1967 when this area was cleared for new housing. Its licence was removed to the Twin Towers, King Edward's Road, Ladywood, which opened in 1971.

80. Three Horseshoes, 231 Summer Lane / Cowper Street, 3.8.1961. This 1860s beerhouse was typical of the twenty or so that were to be found on the street corners off Summer Lane. It was described in a Summer Lane Pubs Memories book as "quiet, non-descript ... not very popular..." The pub closed in 1967 and this side of Cowper Street no longer exists, with housing now occupying this site.

81. New Woolpack, 368 Summer Lane / Henrietta Street, 31.1.1968. This mid Victorian beerhouse was sometimes referred to as the Woolpack Hotel. It was purchased by Ansells from a Mr. S. A. Ward for £500 in 1889 and later rebuilt. Regulars here included a mixture of businessmen and workers from the MEB Power Station that stood opposite. The pub closed at the end of 1968 and its licence was removed to the newly built King of the Road, Hospital Street, which opened in 1971. The Woolpack was demolished, though the other buildings shown have survived and the site today is a car park.

34

Chapter 15 Saltley & Ward End

82. London Tavern, 1 High Street / Crawford Street, 1985. This fully licensed house was purchased freehold by Ansells for £7,000 in 1909. Its licence was revoked 5.8.1999 and the pub has now been demolished. Part of the site is currently occupied by a small car park.

83. Fox & Goose, Washwood Heath Road / Bromford Lane, c1935. This magnificent building replaced an old home-brew, stabling inn back in 1913. It harked back to earlier times, with its Tudor chimneys and latticed windows. The architect was Holland W Hobbis, best known for his churches and schools, but also for the College Arms (see page 22) and M & B's Antelope pub at Sparkhill. It is still trading today.

84. Ye Olde Barley Mow, St. Margaret's Road, Ward End, c1928. This had been in existence when all this area was rural in the eraly 1800s. Ansells bought it in 1912 for £11,800 and rebuilt it in the 1920s. The pub is still trading today.

Chapter 16 Sheldon, Small Heath, Stechford & Yardley

The Wheatsheaf, Coventry Road, Sheldon. Bhm.26.

85. Wheatsheaf, 2225 Coventry Road / Hob's Moat Road, Sheldon c1960, before road widening. Since 2000, the pub has been a Toby Carvery and Lodge, with Mock Tudor wooden panelling now applied to the brick built building. This busy junction is now dominated by a gantry of traffic lights overhanging the road.

86. Bolton Arms, 308 Bolton Road / Oakley Road, c1936. This building was later rebuilt. A former Holt's pub, the Bolton Arms was popular for live music in the 1960s. Its licence was not renewed 9.2.1989 and the building is now in use as a Banqueting Suite. Note the period Ansells signage.

87. Small Arms Inn, 64 Muntz Street / Hawkes Street, c1959. This former Holts Victorian three-storey back street boozer dominated the unremarkable terraced housing of these streets. It closed 11.6.1974 and Small Heath Library now occupies this site. Hawkes Street has been truncated.

88. Tile Cottage, 247 Coventry Road, c1971. This was a small, late Victorian beerhouse, sandwiched between a Co-operative Store and a Travel Agent. Looking somewhat run down, the Cottage closed 1.8.1975 and this whole row of buildings was demolished due to subsequent road widening.

89. Glebe, Glebe Farm Road / Kitt's Green Road, c1936. Note the architectural Tudor references and Dutch gables. It was later renamed Cock'n'Bull before reverting to the Glebe. Its licence was revoked 30.3.2004. Now demolished, this large site has been replaced by a housing estate.

90. Swan, Coventry Road / Yardley Road, c1968. This was at least the third building on the site, having replaced its Victorian (1899) mock Tudor predecessor when the Swan underpass was built. It opened on 24.2.1967. This was the largest pub in the country, boasting eight bars and with a staff of ninety. Its licence was surrendered on 10.7.1989 and now this building has in turn been demolished, replaced by an office block.

Chapter 17 Sparkbrook and Sparkhill

91. Gate Inn, 14 Studley Street, Sparkbrook, c1936, when Frank Niblett was licensee of this former Holts Victorian beerhouse. Note the faded, painted Holts sign for Malt Ales and the ornate lanterns. Its licence was revoked 5.8.1999 and the building has survived, now as a function room hire venue.

92. Royal Oak, 31 Alfred Street / 69 Stoney Lane, Sparkbrook, 1985. This former Victorian beerhouse with a dual address, seen here with classic Ansells signage is still open today.

93. Shakespeare, 56 & 58 Stratford Road / Henley Street, 1953. This former beerhouse dates from the mid nineteenth century. This scene was captured by the great transport photographer, D J Norton on the last day of the trams. A scene not greatly changed today, minus the tram, of course!

94. Mermaid Hotel, Stratford Road / Warwick Road, 1972. There has been a pub at this important and busy junction since at least the 1750s. The current building dates from the 1930s and suffered bomb damage. It closed in 1992 to become a restaurant but has subsequently suffered fire damage.

95. Sportsman, 79 Warwick Road / Shakespeare Street, 1985. This striking red brick Jacobean-style pub dates from c1900 in James & Lister Lea style of architecture. It replaced an earlier beerhouse. Back in the 1970s, it lived up to its name offering pool, table football, darts and tele-tennis in the bar! It is still open for trading, renamed Majors, then from 2004, McDwyers.

Chapter 18 Winson Green & Brookfields

96. Sir Robert Peel, 99 Peel Street, c1967. This two-storey former beerhouse was smaller than the surrounding terraced houses. Its licence was surrendered in 1977. All buildings in the street have now been replaced by modern housing.

97. Cottage of Content, 59 Norman Street / Carlisle Street. This former beerhouse is pictured towards its demise in April 1978, shortly before it called time in June of that year. The replacement housing can just be seen to the right of the pub.

98. Old College Inn, 167 & 9 Spring Hill / College Street, c1968. In the 1860s, it was recorded as the College Inn. It was last orders for this former Holts three storey pub when it closed for demolition in 1970. Housing now occupies this site, albeit set much further back from the main road.